# DEPRESSION

Felix M.T. Wong

# DEPRESSION

STEVEN W. SPOTTS, PSY.D.

Rapha Publishing/Word Inc.

Houston and Dallas, TX

**Depression**
by Steven W. Spotts, Psy.D.

© 1991 by Rapha, Inc.

Scripture quotations are from the NEW AMERICAN
STANDARD BIBLE © The Lockman Foundation,
1960, 1962, 1963, 1968, 1971, 1972, 1973, 1975,
1977.

Second Printing, 1992
ISBN:   0-945276-24-9
Printed in the United States of America

# CONTENTS

FOREWORD .................................................................. vii

WHAT IS DEPRESSION? ............................................... 1

CHRISTIAN ATTITUDES .................................................. 7

WHO GETS DEPRESSED? ............................................. 15

WHAT CAUSES DEPRESSION? .................................... 23

WHAT DOES DEPRESSION LOOK LIKE? ................. 31

TYPICAL RESPONSES TO DEPRESSION .................... 35

WHAT TYPES OF HELP ARE AVAILABLE

    FOR DEPRESSION? .............................................. 41

APPENDIX ................................................................... 59

# FOREWORD

Many Christians have experienced depression personally, but they know little about it formally. This booklet seeks to inform the Christian community of the symptoms and underlying processes characteristic of depression. The intent is to help foster a supportive community of informed Christians where people feel free to grow and legitimate healing from depression can actively take place.

# WHAT IS DEPRESSION?

Depression is normal—even for a Christian. Now there's a depressing thought for you. If you are experiencing a severe depression currently (or are close to someone who is) you may be asking, *You mean this miserable blackness, this pit of despair, this desperation and hopelessness I feel (or see in another) is normal?* Well, not exactly. It all depends on what we mean by *normal*. One of the things that makes the subject of depression so difficult is that it covers a broad spectrum of different identifiable symptoms played out in a variety of patterns. In view of this difficulty, let's backtrack a little.

Most of us have been or will be depressed if we live long enough, even though we all try to avoid it. Times have changed. Unlike our own day, to be melancholic in certain cultural settings of the 17th and 18th centuries was a status symbol. Historically, descriptions of depression have even been found in ancient Egyptian odes and poems preserved on papyri, as well as in scriptural accounts of Old Testament characters dating to Cain (Gen. 4:6).

Dejection, gloom, and self-depreciation are common symptoms of depression. In more severe forms (often called *clinical depression*), bodily functions are impaired so that constant fatigue and either too much or too little sleep are common. As we will see later in this booklet, the causes of depression can be physiological (such as a tumor or influenza), but the two most common causes are repressed anger and a deep sense of loss.

Depression takes many forms and exists in differing degrees. The vast majority of us experience periods of depression that are relatively mild. It affects our productivity and efficiency in performing various functions in life only minimally, if at all. In fact, many in this condition probably would not even admit to being depressed. The only noticeable symptoms may be a grumpier attitude than usual, a temporary change in eating or sleeping habits, withdrawal from others, and feelings of apathy toward issues and concerns that might otherwise be considered important.

Periods of depressed mood often are precipitated by some sort of loss . . . the loss of a job, a relationship, a dream, or even a material possession. The milder forms of mood changes that result are common and generally require no treatment per se. When a person's environment is relatively supportive, and an individual has some measure of control over the course of life events, his or her depressive feelings even may go unnoticed.

On the other hand, moderate and severe forms of depression are harder to ignore—both by those who experience them directly and by those who are in contact with the sufferer. These more serious states of depression may be due to the fact that environmental or interpersonal means of support are unavailable or are countersupportive, or in some cases may be the result of long-term disappointment with the limited support available. Individuals with inadequate or depleted resources or support systems are left with little control over finding ways to replace their loss, and thus experience increased depressive symptoms. Many families do not foster honesty about painful emotions. Instead of experiencing comfort, love, and understanding, people in these families learn to suppress these painful feelings. When hurt and anger are suppressed for many months or years, both depression and outbursts of anger can occur.

Other contributing or causative factors for those that suffer from more severe forms of depression might include a genetic predisposition or a biochemical imbalance in the basic transmitting substances of the brain.

# CHRISTIAN ATTITUDES

If you are a Christian you might be thinking, *But I thought Christians were not supposed to suffer from these kinds of problems. Aren't we supposed to have victory over depression?* As Christians, we have been supported in this view by a number of Christian leaders and perhaps even by friends and acquaintances. People that you respect may have led you to believe that "depressed Christians" are a contradiction in terms and poor recommendations for the Gospel. Christian speakers and authors sometimes imply that it is always a spiritual deficiency in a person that leads to depression. Even our friends may tell us that being depressed means we are not trusting God or doing what we should be doing for Him.

This approach fails to take into account significant passages found in the Scriptures. In the book of Job, the Lord speaks to Satan and says, "Have you considered My servant Job? For there is no one like him on the earth, a blameless and upright man, fearing God and turning away from evil" (Job 1:8). This is quite a recommendation. There hardly seems to be much lacking in the way of God-pleasing spirituality in Job's life. However, it would be hard to argue that Job was not depressed when he said, "And now my soul is poured out within me; days of affliction have seized me. At night it pierces my bones within me, and my gnawing pains take no rest" (Job 30:16-17).

In the book of Lamentations, the prophet Jeremiah laments the sorrows of Judah and says of himself: "...my soul has been rejected from peace; I have forgotten happiness. So I say, 'My strength has perished, and so has my hope from the Lord'" (Lam. 3:17-18). Although he also reports finding hope in the ultimate character of God (Lam. 3:21-23), he goes on to say things like, "Panic and pitfall have befallen us..."; "My eyes pour down unceasingly, without stopping..."; and, "The joy of our hearts has ceased; our dancing has been turned into mourning" (Lam. 3:47, 49; 5:15).

Jeremiah was God's righteous prophet. Though he doubtless shared in the sins of the human race, he was not guilty of the idolatry for which Judah was judged by God. Yet he suffered the same judgment for idolatry as did the rest of the nation. In short, he experienced distress precipitated by the sins of others.

This is the case in our day as well. Depression can result from our own poor choices or moral laxity, however, many people also struggle with depression because of actions initiated by others. In addition, we live in a fallen world system that displays a depravity similar to that found in Judah in the days of Jeremiah. All of those who lived in Judah suffered, not just those who were evil.

In our day, many individuals are raised in dysfunctional family systems characterized by addiction, neglect, abuse, and by parents or caretakers who are excessively preoccupied with their own needs. The fact that children who grow up in such homes suffer from depression is not surprising—it is to be expected. However, whether or not the precipitating causes of one's depression are physical, psychological, or spiritual, condemning someone for being depressed is to apply an unsound theology, and perhaps more importantly, to completely miss the flavor of the Gospels. Brennan Manning, in his marvelous book, *Lion and Lamb*, writes,

*The relentless tenderness of Jesus challenges us to give up our false faces, our petty conceits, our irritating vanities, our preposterous pretending, and become card-carrying members of the messy human community. Jesus calls us to be tender with each other because He is tender. He invites us into the fellowship of saved sinners wherein our identity and glory lie not in titles, trinkets, honorary degrees, and imaginary differences but in our 'new self' in Christ irrevocably bonded to our brothers and sisters in the family of God.[1]*

For the Christian who experiences depression, the lack of support he finds within the Christian community can be a particularly disturbing problem. This is not new. Apparently even Job recognized this when he said, "For the despairing man there should

11

be kindness from his friend; lest he forsake the fear of the Almighty" (Job 6:14).

Author Alice Slaikeu Lawhead interviewed 50 women for her book, *The Lie of the Good Life*. Although the responses to her questions were mixed, some struck a chord in me as I compared them to those I observe in my own clinical work.

One woman reports,

*A lot of my Christian friends try to cheer me up. They say, "Hey, everything is going to work out just fine. It all works together for good. You just hang in there and read your Bible and pray, and God will see you through this."*

*They won't let me experience my disappointment. They can't handle the failure of it themselves, and they don't want me to deal with it either. There is this pressure to keep looking okay, like every-thing is going to be all right.*

*But we're not all going to live happily ever after. We aren't going to be okay. Life is hard. It gets rough, and then it gets rougher. It's full of disappoint-ments and disillusionments.*

*Yet some of my friends can't accept this. They keep up with this naive optimism. And it creates tremendous conflict in me. Because I know, deep down, that I am right about life being difficult.*[2]

Yes, life is difficult. There are not al-ways answers to problems. Not everything can be fixed. And when life gets bad, we often feel "down." We grieve our losses. We experience the gloom of depression. This "basic depressed response"[3] is a "normal" human reaction, one which I have come to believe is a God-given emotion necessary for adequate resolution of grief and certain other internal conflicts. What happens after this initial adaptive response is where the supportive Christian community can either play a significant role in the healing process or else unwittingly contribute to a downward spiral of unproductive depression and despair.

Let's take a look at who gets depressed, what causes depression, what depression looks like, typical responses to depression, and what types of help currently are available.

# WHO GETS DEPRESSED?

A recent article described the life of American theologian, Jonathan Edwards (1703-1758). In 1734, Edwards' series of sermons on love from the thirteenth chapter of First Corinthians began the Great Awakening within his Northhampton church. "Scarcely a single person in the whole town was left unconcerned about the great things of the eternal world," Edwards said. Emotions were running wild, and his wife Sarah was caught up in the ecstasy. During a six-month period, some 300 people claimed to have been converted in the small Massachusetts town.

Then, just as quickly as the fervor had exploded, it faded. Many of the townspeople who had claimed a spiritual experience returned to their vices. Edwards was discouraged. What amazed him, however, was what he observed in Sarah. Normally the calm manager, she began to be picky and irritable. Looking back on this period, Edwards later wrote that she was "subject to unsteadiness and many ups and downs...often subject to melancholy."[4]

The article went on to explain that Edwards later was dismissed from his church in controversy, had difficulty finding work, assumed a meager frontier post and died one month after rising to the presidency of Princeton.

The article painted a portrait of the Edwards as very human and realistic. They were not superhuman. Edwards and his wife were godly people, instruments of revival during the Great Awakening. They also were people who experienced discouragement, depression, and defeat when faced with the inevitable difficulties and disappointments of life.

A story is told that Dag Hammerskjold, former secretary-general of the United Nations, once indicated that in spite of his renown, he had considered suicide because his life seemed empty. Apparently, it was only after he began to put as much commitment into his personal relationships as he had put into his career that he again began to find hope.

Many years ago a young midwestern lawyer suffered such a deep depression that his friends thought it wise to keep all knives and razors away from him. During this period he wrote, "I am now the most miserable man living. Whether I shall ever be better, I cannot tell. I awfully forebode I shall not." He was wrong. He recovered from that awfulness we call depression, and went on to become one of America's most beloved president's, Abraham Lincoln.[5]

Don Baker, former pastor of my own church in Portland, wrote the following of his experience with depression: "I seemed to be out of touch with reality. Life was a blur, often out of focus. My life seemed to be nothing but pretense and fantasy. No one really cared, I felt—not even God. The only solution—at times—seemed to be suicide. To be told that Christians never get depressed only pushed me deeper into my black hole of depression."[6]

Some time ago a woman recounted the events in her life that led to her depression. She and her husband had worked for competing corporations. She was called into an office one day where she found her husband, along with some federal officials. They informed her that her husband was going to be charged with felony embezzlement. She told me that she couldn't have been more shocked if she had put her hand in a light socket. Her husband had handled their family finances for years and they both had good incomes. They were putting away money for retirement. When his crime was discovered, all of their assets and accounts were frozen. Their home and cars were forfeited.

In her shock and rage at her betrayal by him she entered a deep depression and began to consider suicide, eventually being hospitalized. During the course of the investigation she was forced to take a polygraph. Although she prided herself on her honesty and integrity, she felt guilty by association. In her depressed state she admitted to an investigator that the worst thing she had ever done was to minimally "pad" her expense account (which she had later paid back). At the time she did not know that this admission was cause for her dismissal from her job. When released from the hospital, she was promptly fired. She had a son in college, a daughter at home, and a husband of 30 years whom she no longer felt she knew. Both were out of work, would have to change careers in their mid-50s, and went, in a few short weeks, from an upper-middle-class American dream to a nightmare in which they had to apply for food stamps and other public assistance. Perhaps it goes without saying that no easy solutions were in sight.

Was this woman's personal experience normal? No. Was her depressive reaction normal? Yes. In fact, she would have been considered abnormal had she not been depressed. She experienced a tremendous sense of loss: the loss of her job, income, family stability, status in the community, self-esteem, and a shock to every aspect of her life. Her feelings of gloom were expressions of her grief, a normal depressive response. Unfortunately, the concept of "normal depression" is not easily accepted.

Studies find that roughly twice as many women as men report an incidence of major depression in their lifetime. One U.S. National Survey indicated that *annually* 2.8 percent of men and 6.9 percent of women suffer a major depressive episode. Culturally, depressed feelings often are perceived as signs of weakness, particularly when found in men, leadership, clergy, or in those otherwise expected to be strong. Historically, depressed feelings have been only slightly better tolerated in women or others considered to be more fragile. However, the truth is that depression is one of the most common responses to which mankind is subject; given the right set of circumstances, everyone experiences it at some level.

# *WHAT CAUSES DEPRESSION?*

The symptoms and signs of depression are multiple and complex; accordingly, so are its causes. In many instances depression takes the obvious form as seen in bereavement or normal grief reactions. When one experiences a loss, or is frustrated in an attempt to reach a desired goal by the use of available personal resources, then a depressive response results. A point made earlier was that depressive symptoms can vary considerably in magnitude, from mild to severe. Mild cases can be mild because the crisis is less severe or because it is resolved efficiently with adequate support. Moderate or severe forms of depres-

23

sion may be due to a more intense crisis, or to biological vulnerabilities in the person experiencing the crisis and a lack of external support for him or her.

The psychological and interpersonal causes of depression are perhaps the most obvious. When we experience a loss, become frustrated in the pursuit of a goal or face rejection from important others, depression is the natural emotional response. Whether or not this natural response then becomes a potentially depressive syndrome depends upon a variety of interacting factors, including one's support systems, personal resources, personal background, and severity of stress, among others.

Internalized anger and the experience of loss have sometimes been viewed as "twin horns" in the cause of depression. It is important to understand how these two ideas relate because one really grows out of the other.

Losses occur in everyone's life, but of course they vary considerably in degree. Some people lose jobs or material possessions, while others may lose a leg to cancer or a close family member to illness or accident. Some people lose their dignity when violated as a victim of crime; some lose their sense of value and security because they grow up in a condemning or neglectful family; and others lose a "once in a lifetime opportunity" to pursue a dream.

We are often prone to categorize these losses according to their severity and then make covert judgments about whether we or another should be depressed about them. We might fail to take into account, however, what has gone on before. What other losses have been experienced? When did they occur? Have the losses been chronic or only occasional? What type of support was offered at the time? Were we allowed to experience the fullness of our loss at the time, or did we have to pretend that we were really okay?

It is not only the severity of the actual loss itself that is important to judge when attempting to understand what causes a depression; rather, it is the individual's *perception* of that loss and the meaning assigned to it. When people repeatedly experience the world as hostile and rejecting, or cold, disinterested, and unsupportive, these experiences shape their view of themselves and others. For instance, they may come to believe that they are responsible when anything goes wrong, or when anyone is unhappy. Others will have difficulty trusting offers of legitimate help because they have never been able to trust anyone without getting hurt in the process. This sometimes leads to the feeling that *I can't tell anyone how I feel because they really don't care, and they would probably just blame me anyway*.

The anger and frustration we feel when experiencing a loss is then turned inward. Eventually, we become bad in our own eyes, unable to see in ourselves any of the image or likeness of God in which we were created. We may feel false guilt, shame, humiliation, vulnerability, or helplessness, finally leading to feelings of hopelessness. At this point, some feel the compulsion to kill themselves, as though suicide is the only thing that makes sense. They want to permanently do away with what is bad. Others feel suicidal because their internalized anger begins "leaking out," and they desperately want some way to let important others know just how angry they really are.

Anger is internalized because of the repeated failure of others to allow for it's normal expression. This anger becomes the self-directed hate which is found in depressive symptoms such as suicidal impulses, or a variety of other self-abusive behaviors.

Depression is not only the result of loss and internalized anger. It can also be due to a variety of biological or physiological precipitators. In these cases, the more common causes of depression are absent, and the depressive symptoms are often ignored. For example, some medications can bring on a depressive episode with or without a psychosocial stressor. This is particularly true of certain medications used to control high blood pressure. Various diseases such as lymphoma or pancreatic cancer or tumors in certain locations may initiate a depression before the individual is aware of it. One of my professors was fond of recounting a story concerning a missionary he had treated who suffered from a severe depression that had caused her to return from the mission field. After a month of tests and therapy, a CT (computed tomography) scan was ordered, and a tumor was discovered. Fortunately, the tumor was removed intact and her depression was resolved immediately.

At times depression may occur following an illness such as hepatitis, infectious mononucleosis, and influenza. Some women suffer from severe, pre-menstrual depression in which mood swings, anger, and suicidal thoughts are common. Even changes in the season and the amount of sunlight are thought to cause some depressions known as "seasonal affective disorders."

In addition to physiological circumstances that may precipitate depression, there is considerable evidence that genetic factors play a role in predisposing people to depressive illness. This is particularly true of the more severe depressive disorders. This means that if a person's family history includes evidence of severe depression, he may be more prone to experience similar episodes than the general population.

# *WHAT DOES DEPRESSION LOOK LIKE?*

Diagnostically there are a number of specific types of mood disorders although, as was already stated, depressive symptoms may occur in a variety of other situations and in combination with other ailments. Depressive episodes characterized by symptoms of depressed mood or loss of interest and pleasure in most of life's activities may represent the more typical understanding of depression. Additional symptoms which represent a more severe depression may include weight loss or gain; too little or too much sleep; noticeable agitation or slowed functioning; fatigue and loss of energy;

feelings of worthlessness and/or guilt; problems in concentrating and making decisions; and, suicidal thoughts or plans. This major type of depression can occur either as a single episode or can recur periodically, and when very severe can include symptoms like delusions or hallucinations. Less severe but chronic episodes are called "dysthymia."

Certain types of depression can appear to be just the opposite of what one might expect. These are called "bipolar depressions," in which the pole opposite of the depressed phase is experienced or observed as a persistent mood that is elevated or excessively irritable. This is a manic phase during which one may exhibit several of the following symptoms: inflated self-esteem or a belief that he can do almost anything; a decreased need for sleep; a tendency to monopolize conversations; difficulty in organizing racing thoughts; distractibility; increased activity affecting work, school, social life, or sexuality; and, behaviors which may be pleasurable but which are likely to have painful consequences. Symptoms of a manic phase may interfere markedly with occupational functioning, social activities, and/or important relationships. Once again, in severe cases, a person may experience delusional thinking or hallucinations and lose touch with reality.

Some bipolar disorders manifest both manic and depressed phases, but others may reveal only the manic phase or the depressed phase. Although one who is experiencing a mild manic state can be charming and productive, when the disorder increases in severity, friends and family members may begin to suffer as well. Occasionally, manic episodes are of a lesser degree and the sufferer seems to cycle in and out of both manic and depressed states. These chronic but milder states of mania and depression are called "cyclothymia."

Sometimes depressive symptoms are associated with significant psychological or social stressors but never develop into a true depressive syndrome. These typically are called "adjustment disorders" and simply describe a relatively short-term impairment in work, school, or relationships which is directly related to a difficult life situation. The adjustment may involve a variety of emotional and/or behavioral reactions that exceed what one might expect of someone in that situation. At times this will include a depressive response such as a depressed mood, tearfulness, or feelings of hopelessness.

# *TYPICAL RESPONSES TO DEPRESSION*

Symptoms of depression often are complicated by other emotions and behavioral attempts to compensate for, or avoid, depressive feelings. In addition to a subjective sense of depression, depressed individuals can feel angry, anxious, arrogant, bitter, bored, confused, cynical, fearful, guilty, shameful, hopeless, hapless, and/or helpless. They frequently engage in activities designed to limit or resolve their feelings of depression but which actually contribute to their continuation. For example, a common response to feeling depressed is to buy something new. When one has the resources to do so, this may not cause a problem. In fact, it may temporarily relieve the sufferer's subjective sense of feeling depressed. However, if the sufferer exceeds his or her resources and is confronted by a collection agency due to bad debts, then his or her depression may return with an even greater intensity.

Other behaviors in which the necessary work of depression is set aside for a temporary respite from painful feelings include the compulsive use of alcohol, drugs, tobacco, food, sex, television, telephone, money, or any other substance, object, or person leading to destructive consequences. These compulsive behaviors can be thought of as an individual's attempt to ward off a depressive state by repeatedly performing some act that supplants his or her depressive feelings with something relatively more pleasurable. In addition, failure to adequately work through legitimate depression leads some to literally pull their hair out.

Compulsive hair-pulling (trichotillomania) is generally considered a depressive equivalent. It primarily is found in young adolescent or preadolescent girls, although occasionally adults will gradually break off hairs at the scalp, sometimes leaving large areas of thinned or missing hair.

Physical complaints are common in many depressions and this further complicates the picture. Depression is not always apparent when a person complains of stomachaches or tension in the neck and head, however, this can be the case. Problems with sleeping, appetite, digestion, weight, constipation, sexual urges, bodily fatigue, and pain all are associated rather frequently with depressive illnesses. Although these signs generally are thought to result from a depressive episode, they also play a causative role in its continuance.

Age adds to the complexity of identifying depression. Depression often is manifested differently at different ages. Infants, for example, can experience what is known as "anaclitic depression." When babies are deprived of the attentions of their mother (or primary caregiver), they initially will cry and refuse the care of another. After a time they will settle down and their distress will appear to have diminished. In reality they are experiencing a state of mourning. Infants who have not been reconnected with their primary caretakers have been known to waste away and die in this condition. More typically, when mom or the primary parent returns, the child initially will want nothing to do with her, as if to say in angry dependence, *I don't need you, but you had better never do that to me again!*

In our household, my wife and I exert considerable effort to get our three children to talk about how they feel, but sometimes the best they can do is say, "I don't feel so good." Children who are significantly depressed at the grade-school age-level find it particularly difficult to express their feelings of despair, and instead may demonstrate a variety of "acting-out behaviors," including hyperactivity, fire-setting, accident tendencies, or bed-wetting. While children always will exhibit some negative behaviors, one should raise the suspicion of depression if one observes continual sulking, clinging, an inability to tolerate being separated from someone for a time, attacks of weeping or sadness, self-deprecation, a lack of interest in things, or withdrawal and isolation from the rest of the family.

Adolescents have a greater capacity to talk about what they feel, but if depressed, they may become antisocial in an attempt to express their despair. Unfortunately, when this is met by a lack of understanding and/or severe punishment meted out by a hostile adult world, the depression likely will intensify.

Throughout adult development, depressions may result from numerous difficulties in relating to others or working effectively.

The challenges of intimacy, career, marital conflicts, parenting, the empty nest, retirement, and death of loved ones all can bring on periods of depression. It is not uncommon for the elderly to seek out physicians to discuss physical complaints, perhaps in part because they do not know how else to express their need for help with depressed feelings, and/or because the responsive or supportive social systems necessary for their well-being aren't available to them.

# WHAT TYPES OF HELP ARE AVAILABLE FOR DEPRESSION?

If you have experienced any of the above symptoms, or know someone who has, you probably are wondering what kind of help is available. Before I offer some possibilities, let's consider what doesn't help.

It often is difficult to find people who can keep their cool when those around them are losing theirs. The tendency to feel uncomfortable when friends or family members are experiencing depressed feelings can lead us to make serious errors in our attempts to help. Perhaps most common is the sense that we need to "fix" what is bothering them. This inclination implies that we really understand their problems, when in fact we may not be able to tolerate their discomfort long enough or deeply enough to emphatically share in their experience of it. Secondly, assuming that we can fix what someone else has perhaps been struggling with for quite some time is presumptuous. It is far too common for a "would-be helper" to provide a list of "justs" for the sufferer, such as, "Just trust God to help you," or, "Just look on the bright side and be positive about this." Worse yet are comments like, "If you just hadn't taken that job..." To the sufferer, these types of comments either appear arrogant and increase his sense of anger and despair, or they make him feel even more like a failure than he does already.

Another variety of input that is not helpful falls into what I call, the "it-could-be-worse" category. Such statements include, "If you would just get out and help somebody else you would get your mind off of your own problems," or, "I remember when that happened to me," or, "Just be thankful you..." or, "At least you didn't..." Sometimes we share our own experiences with depression and give a prescription for how we "conquered" it. The implication is that the depressed person really should be thankful (rather than depressed) either because he could have had it worse or because someone else does. Comparing one person's pain to another's usually is unproductive. It doesn't lessen the sufferer's subjective sense of pain and leads to even greater feelings of alienation, guilt, and despair. The result is that the person who suffers feels that nobody really understands him or her.

What does help?

1. *Give others freedom to experience their own feelings.* Encourage them to express "feelings states," even depressive ones, rather than trying to talk them out of those feelings.

When we are feeling badly, it is not uncommon for someone to tell us, "I don't

43

think you should feel that way," and then attempt to argue with us about how we are "supposed" to feel. If we then attempt to import the feelings others tell us we "should" have, we can lose the sense of how we really feel.

2. *See depression as a meaningful work necessary for adequate resolution of certain internal dynamics.* For instance, in a depression resulting from the loss of a loved object (a person, possession, or dream), the "internal dynamic" is one of determining whether and how one can replace that love object, given one's current resources. In this sense, depression is not something to be avoided at all costs. In fact, given the right type of supportive environment, and in an effort to avoid creating longstanding problems, depression is an important work that should be encouraged. Obviously, some "objects" never can be replaced, such as the loss of

a normal childhood (for an adult survivor of abusive or neglectful parents), or the death of a loved one. Time cannot be turned back any more than a sin-scarred world can be made harmless. However, unless a person is allowed to grieve such real losses effectively, he may spend a lifetime in a depressed or depressed-like state, unable to achieve any productive internal resolution.

3. *Realize that anyone who really is beginning to deal with loss is likely to experience an increase in depressive symptoms*. This prospect often frightens both the depressed person and those who may be attempting to help—but it need not. Such an increase may result from an increased sense of safety created by adequate support, a corresponding reduction of personal defenses, and an attempt to begin dealing honestly with an inner reality. Therefore, an increase in

depressive feelings does not mean you are doing something wrong. Instead, it may be a sign that you are on the right track.

4. *Although depressed individuals may have experienced severe losses in the past, they need to know that others care about them now*. Meaningful relationships and connections give people a reason to live. Therefore, helping depressed people usually involves establishing a meaningful connection with them and helping them recall other important relationships which have been sustaining them. Essentially, this is a way of establishing a balanced perspective by focusing specifically on the resources available to them.

5. *Understand that it is not depressive feelings that harm people, but the actions they may take to avoid those feelings*. Drug and alcohol abuse sometimes can

be viewed as an attempt to self-medicate, or relieve, feelings of depression without ever adequately understanding and facing their causes. Those of us who attempt to help often unwittingly encourage such an avoidance by focusing on short-term symptom reduction at the expense of adequate resolution. While we may need to intervene so that destructive actions do not have permanent consequences, we must not forget that they only are symptoms of an underlying process. The tragic result of our failure to understand this may be untold physical, emotional, and spiritual harm due to grief that is never resolved.

In summary, effective help for depressed individuals must come from a person or community that can tolerate depressed feelings. Occasionally, this is difficult because there are times when a person's individual level of functioning is vitally important to the overall well-being of others. For instance, when the pastor of a church, the president of a company, or a single parent with three children is depressed, his or her symptoms can have dreadful consequences for those who are depending on that individual's leadership. In some cases of severe depression, a person's life may be in danger because of suicide risk or behavior that reflects a loss of touch with reality. In cases such as these, providing for the patient's safety and prompt symptomatic relief are essential.

Sometimes, despite our best efforts, the depression is too severe for non-professionals. Hospital-based programs designed to treat severe depressive disorders and new advances in medications have made recovery possible for a great many people. Hospital programs can do for a person what family members or friends are often unable to do: provide 24-hour-a-day care at the height of a depressive crisis. In addition, over 20 antidepressant medications now are available which offer few side effects, are usually tolerable, and which provide relatively quick symptomatic relief (within two to three weeks normally). These medications have been found effective in up to 80 percent of depressions and can be targeted for specific types of depression, based on the particular drug action. For some people, however, medications either do not work or would be inadvisable for a variety of medical reasons. One particular advantage of hospital-based programs is that medications can be monitored carefully for effect while other types of therapeutic treatments proceed.

Whether or not medications are to be used depends on a number of factors which must be evaluated by medical and psychological personnel. For the Christian seeking relief from depression, the thought of using psychoactive medications may be troublesome. However, fears of becoming addicted or dependent on these medications are unfounded. They do not artificially produce a "high" which creates a greater need for the drug.

49

The basic mechanism for most of these medications is that they help the brain restore chemical resources necessary for effective functioning. (See the Appendix for further explanation of how these medications work to relieve depression.)

Of course, medications alone cannot resolve the precipitating causes of one's depression. Although they have been found to be very helpful in some instances, other types of therapies are equally important and should be considered in order to help people achieve a productive end to their depression. Individual or group therapy with a mental-health professional who understands depressive illnesses and works effectively with them may be important. Ideally, this person also should understand how a person's spiritual life both affects and is affected by depression. Finding the right person to help sometimes is difficult, but usually pastors or other professionals have access to referral networks. If you are depressed, I hope that you will have the courage to ask for help.

God created us as relational beings and our relational connections give us reason for living. Therefore, our relationship with God, our family, friends, co-workers, and church all play a significant role in the healing process. If such individuals or groups are supportive, then much is to be gained from interaction with them, even though we may feel like withdrawing. If they are not supportive, then it will be important to find new sources of support. However, when in a depressive crisis, it usually is not a good time to make major changes or decisions without some counsel from one or more individuals who are mature, trustworthy, and objective. Too often, people overwhelmed by failed or failing relationships permanently close doors on other relationships. An impulsive change, such as moving, getting married or divorced, or changing employers or churches, probably is not going to help us achieve a productive end to our depression, and the long-term effects of such a change could be devastating. Therefore, major life changes should be implemented carefully, with a full understanding of their probable consequences.

Sometimes milder forms of depression can be helped by a personal examination of our thought processes. What we say to ourselves about ourselves, about God, and about others often can be a distortion based on lack of information or, worse yet, misinformation. I know of one fellow who became depressed because he heard that "Patti" (his girlfriend from the prior year at school) was dating somebody else. When he later mentioned this to one of his friends, he learned that it wasn't "his Patti" but another Patti. This new information allowed for a quick recovery from his feelings of rejection, even though he never actually went out with Patti again.

In other instances, misinformation is not so easily corrected. Distorted thoughts can be etched so deeply into our cognitive processes that it takes mounds of contrary evidence to rectify them. Even then, some people will steadfastly hold to these distortions in spite of the evidence. Nevertheless, this tendency suggests why it is so important to be continually exposed to the truth about God as found in the Bible.

The prophet Isaiah comforted the troubled people of Jerusalem by saying,

> *"Comfort, O comfort My people," says your God. "Speak kindly to Jerusalem; and call out to her, that her warfare has ended, . . . ."*

Is. 40:1, 2a

Remember, Isaiah's words were prophetic. These people were still to be carried into captivity and suffer many hardships, however, the Lord speaks to His people as to lambs,

53

*Like a shepherd He will tend*
*His flock, in His arm He will*
*gather the lambs, and carry them*
*in His bosom; He will gently lead*
*the nursing ewes.*

Is. 40:11

God cares for His people even when He is accused of neglecting them.

After recounting the power and magnificence of God, Isaiah asks Israel why they say God does not understand them and that He does not care about the injustices done to them. In response, he corrects their thinking:

*Do you not know? Have you*
*not heard? The Everlasting God,*
*the Lord, the Creator of the ends*
*of the earth does not become weary*
*or tired. His understanding is*
*inscrutable.*

*He gives strength to the weary, and to him who lacks might He increases power.*

*Though youths grow weary and tired, and vigorous young men stumble badly,*

*Yet those who wait for the Lord will gain new strength; they will mount up with wings like eagles, they will run and not get tired, they will walk and not become weary.*

Is. 40:28-31

This does not mean you will never get tired or that feeling depressed or discouraged reflects a lack of faith on your part. In fact, it acknowledges these feelings as part of normal experience. This passage indicates that hope is essential to strength. As hope waxes and wanes, so does our strength. Fortunately, our ultimate hope is in a God who does not change, who understands us and who cares for us as a tender shepherd cares for his lambs, and who will one day make right all the injustice that has been done. This is why another prophet very familiar with the feelings of depression (He may have written the first book about it—called the Lamentations of Jeremiah.) wrote,

> *This I recall to my mind,*
> *Therefore I have hope.*
> *The Lord's lovingkindnesses*
> *indeed never cease, for His*
> *compassions never fail.*
> *They are new every morn-*
> *ing; Great is Thy faithfulness.*

Lam. 3:21-23

Most of us have spent too many years in the darkness, hiding in fear, lest we be exposed for being human. Pretending not to be depressed because it makes one feel abnormal or unacceptable is not the answer for the Christian. Our thoughts, feelings, and behaviors all must be brought out into the light if we are to experience healing. This means allowing others (and ourselves) to be where they are and who they are so that they can be free to truly heal and grow. Those who have experienced depression may need to experience a whopping dose of "grace" from others before they will be ready or willing to do this.

While depression sometimes will get better without any type of formal treatment, many times the skills of both medical and mental-health professionals are necessary to provide relief. Whatever the situation, we all need the courage to "walk in the light" so that we can see the truth about ourselves and effectively deal with it. Otherwise, our health, our families, our social relationships, and our spiritual lives will suffer.

# *APPENDIX*
## BY DR. MICHAEL LYLES

In Major Depression Disorder (MDD), the neurotransmitters are deficient in amount, and the areas where they connect (the receptor sites) are also malfunctioning. In this type of depression, one begins to have difficulty with a number of physical and psychological symptoms due to the malfunctioning of the neuronal mechanism in this part of the brain. These symptoms include increases or decreases in sleep or appetite, crying spells, constipation, fatigue, decreases in sexual drive, anxiety, worry, decreased interest in usually pleasurable or fun activities, memory or concentration difficulties, and/or social withdrawal. One's motivation level and zest for life may start to slacken, and thoughts of hopelessness and helplessness can become so prominent that thoughts of suicide become recurrent mental visitors.

There are a number of antidepressant medications which are available for the treatment of MDD. These medications correct the underlying chemical imbalances and receptor problems. These medications take several weeks to work on an average because they are adjusting very delicate systems in the brain. These drugs are not addictive and do not make the person feel "high"—just normal.

Many Christians fear that taking an antidepressant would impair their ability to resolve their problems spiritually or emotionally. To the contrary, depressed persons find that the alleviation of their depression frees them to address problems more clearly and completely. Many depressed

Christians, who do not seek or accept treatment, may become involved in alcohol or drug abuse in an attempt to treat themselves. Many others ruminate about suicide and hopelessness so much that movement in therapy becomes impossible.

Editor's note:

At Rapha, we believe that small groups can provide a nurturing and powerful environment to help people deal with real-life problems such as depression, grief, fear, eating disorders, chemical dependency, codependency, and all kinds of other relational and emotional difficulties. The warmth, honesty, and understanding in those groups helps us understand why we feel and act the way we do. And with the encouragement of others, we can take definitive steps toward healing and health for ourselves and our relationships.

Not all groups, however, provide this kind of "greenhouse" for growth. Some only perpetuate the guilt and loneliness by giving quick and superficial solutions to the deep and often complex problems in our lives.

We urge you to find a group of people in your church, or in a church near you, where the members provide acceptance, love, honesty, and encouragement. Rapha has many different books, workbooks, leader's guides, and types of training so that people in these groups can be nurtured in the love and grace of God and focused on sound biblical principles to help them experience healing and growth.

To obtain a free list of the materials we have available, please write to us at:

Rapha, Inc.
8876 Gulf Freeway, Suite 340
Houston, TX 77017

# REFERENCES

1.  Brennan Manning, *Lion and Lamb* (Old Tappan, N.J.: Fleming H. Revell, 1986), pp. 131-32.

2.  Alice Slaikeu Lawhead, *The Lie of the Good Life* (Portland, OR: Multnomah Press, 1989), p. 270.

3.  Emmy Gut, *Productive and Unproductive Depression* (New York: Basic Books, 1989).

4. B. Peterson, "Sarah and Jonathan Edwards. An Uncommon Union" *Christianity Today*, May/June, 1987, p. 43.

5. P.L. Tan, *Encyclopedia of 7700 Illustrations* (Rockville, MD: Assurance, 1979).

6. Don Baker and E. Nester, *Depression* (Portland, OR: Multnomah Press, 1983).

## ABOUT THE AUTHOR...

**Steven W. Spotts, Psy. D.** received a Master of Arts in Biblical Studies from Dallas Theological Seminary and a doctorate in Clinical Psychology from Western Conservative Baptist Seminary. He is currently a therapist in Portland, Oregon working with adult children of alcoholics and others who suffer from depression.